# The Red Envelope

## University of Central Florida
## Contemporary Poetry Series

# The
# RED
# ENVELOPE

*poems by*

*CarolAnn Russell*

University Presses of Florida

University of Central Florida Press

Orlando

Library of Congress Cataloging in
Publication data appear at end of book

# Acknowledgments

Acknowledgment is made to the following journals and anthologies for poems, or earlier versions of poems, published in them:

*Calliope*: Damages, A Difficult River
*Chariton Review*: Ibeji, Burning the Sweatlodge
*Columbia*: Photo of Women Plowing
*Cutbank*: Crossing the Lake with My Father, Memory of Trees, La Chingada, Plain in Level Grass, For All You Know, Roses, Lilacs, Poppies
*Devil's Millhopper*: Understanding Tornadoes, The Dream Pony
*Intro 10*: Sophia Apollonia
*Laurel Review*: Night for Feeding
*Louisville Review*: A Vase of Flowers
*Midwest Quarterly*: Solitary Song for Black Brother Gone Home
*Missouri Poets Anthology*: What I Said
*Montana Review*: Autumn Parallax
*New Jersey Poetry Journal*: The Talking Doll
*Ohio Review*: News from All Directions, Things We Talk about at Home
*Ploughshares*: Fishing
*Poet & Critic*: Abandoned Farm, The Train Always Goes Home
*Poetry Northwest*: Into the Forest, into the Heart, So Long, The Colors
*Portland Review*: A Real Man of No Titles
*Sonora Review*: The Secret Boats

*The Sound of a Few Leaves*: Plain in Level Grass
*Tendril*: The Brown-headed Cowbird Has a Blue, Blue
   Tongue
*Willow Springs*: What I Said
*Bulletin of the Poetry Society of America*: News from All
   Directions
*Rain in the Forest, Light in the Trees: An Anthology of
   Northwest Poets:* Into the Forest, into the Heart, Au-
   tumn Parallax
*Where We Are: The Montana Poets Anthology*: Crossing the
   Lake with My Father, Fishing, Memory of Trees

I wish to thank the late Richard Hugo for his inspiration,
Madeline DeFrees for her encouragement, and Henry
Carlisle for his suggestions. I am also grateful to Ethe-
ridge Knight, for hearing my voice and Art Homer, for
his support of this manuscript.

# Contents

[ vii ]

[ ix ]

*In memory of my father,*
*Norman Eugene Russell*
*1925–1971*

but now, the window closed, it called again, two-
noted, purple, up-scale, a question, a questioning
demand. this was inside all right, and stayed
inside, sharp, purple as a vein. but as she

got used to it, stopped trembling at it, it
changed her now, returning from day to day,
sometimes a five-noted down-scale, sometimes a
saffron bruise ascending, she could see

quite clearly how at its first daggering out
she had thought it might be pear tree calling
to her or the red-berried bush, a call coming from
crossed branches or red red drops on a plant.

(from "Epiphany" by Leonard Wallace Robinson)

I

## Crossing the Lake with My Father

### I

In clear light of summer, I gather in
armloads of soft purple, white.
I dream a river, the cloud around my body
a lake of ash. To see you clear of death
is not enough, the bridal wreath
endlessly braiding, the lover's swing
gaping. The forgotten kiss, forgotten.
All the purple cut from the trellis.
Flowers drop their petals and night
slides its bolt clean into our bones.
The door opens in, out, and we are alone.

I see you as a young man saying goodbye
to your brothers. A hand moves the blood's
full weight, open, waving. You planted your feet
like corn, your right arm swinging high.

### II

Old women, their freckled hands, exotic shellfish
in the sea of evening. When storms move down
the Gallatin, they perch like crows,
shuffling their ancient cards. They never forget
the chair not empty, when war brought
its glory wreath. You are there,
under the dripping birch, wrapped

kaleidoscope of leaves. A day of dedication,
the bandage hidden. Beside the Nazarene Church
I make your bed, press the soft white robe
against your mouth.

III

Memorial Day. A storm threatens the parade
and out back, Mother takes pictures. Then
we are moving. You, the sailor buoyed
by a cloud of flags. You told me secrets.
Aunt Olive served potatoes in a flowered bowl
hand-painted by a German. The way we carry blood,
slow. The invisible shock of snow. The fall
through a century, steady ghost, the even
touch that never melts the tongue.

I believe I belonged in the car when it crashed,
the white line frozen in my mind, your words
a river I still drown in. You are always
on the wrong side. Now a lake, Now a letter
mailed across an ocean. I lose you again,
the sea exploding in your brain, the alphabet
gone mute as shrapnel.

IV

Father, I was the unfaithful one. The long
grass sweetened for your mowing.
I played only hymns when you were dying,
the motion of my hands like birds
on their lake of keys. We lie humming

[ 4 ]

in the deep. Now walking on water,
sleep in the belly of the whale.
Shells of our former selves hug
the shore, breath
and lap of lake water, slow
river, the subtle slap
of midday bath. Listen.
We are crossing the lake.

## Things We Talk about at Home

Doors opening to no one, automatic writing.
The poltergeist understands
the disappearance of things
until we turn to what we thought was there.
Air invites us and we go.
We follow it like Jesus.

One hot July nothing kept the lawn
from turning brown. There was a war on
somewhere. Some fathers went there.
Bud Mack joined Jaycees and ran the rodeo.
Memorizing sin along the irrigation
ditch from town.
Things happen sometimes

the way water goes on with its life and ours
pulling the dark beyond.
The living room on Willow Street
after the funeral, flows.
Kind relatives,
hands folded like bird wings
around nothing but air.
Suicide, the family word for sad.
While we were sleeping
the river rose without our knowing.

## A Difficult River

turns deep
becoming what we fear
we cannot swim.
In Dakota father swam
brown water. I heard him
talking in his sleep—
river sounds
praying he would find
a way with current.

Mother flowed with another power,
wild girl flowering
at the water's edge. When summer boils
hidden parts of the body
she is the tree I dive from.

Strict water
and the secret, slippered fish
dancing what I barely remember—
heel and toe among rocks.

## The Colors

Because fathers come back
from war
with the unspoken
because mothers burn
their blue dresses of grief,
in the sandbox we dig trenches
for survivors
who follow us nightly from supper.
Imperceptible as stars the ants
come out, dotting the toy tractor.

We try to love the ants
and when we fail we kill them
shrinking like our fathers
to music mothers hum
brushing their hair
or hanging out clothes.
Sundays the nearly invisible
fathers wear grey, brown, and green,
fatigued with hymns
while mothers waddle
in brilliant magenta, cooing our names.

The uniform whites of our eyes
propel the parade of fathers

to the cemetery, its stone markers.
*Hush, someone is praying.*
We are swimming in the sound,
blood spun out of us. We become modern

and sad. In a brick house
on Black Street my father goes out
to gaze at the sun. *Come back.*
He flickers and returns,
agitated bird
gripping the pistol's steel branch,
his man's arm flapping.
White skin my mother kissed sometimes
when he stepped from the bath
her lips wet for days
after the veteran's representative
together with the orderly
took him away, arms tied
like pale wings
straining against the canvas sleeve.
Paint me, Father, turning
blue in the salty womb
as you circle
toward the open door
and dance, dumbly,
into the yard.

You never killed a bird
or hung it like an offering

beside our garage.
The deer roped to the '57 Pontiac's hood
you brought down for food.
I remember the blood on your clothes,
how patiently Mother tied
the neat white packages.
One by one she unwrapped them
learning how to cook and serve
the wild meat.

We share the supper.
Beached near La Push we come close.
Waves bruise us
with their colorless explosions.
Lovers, we repeat the blow,
bread to the insect congregation
honoring the dead—
miscarried, cared for.

## So Long

Goodbye was all my father said
for years. People knew it mattered
when he'd pump their hands, shifting
weight like a wounded buck.
He'd look right through them to the sun
the slow smile of a man who kept his friends,
eyes blue behind the squint. Like some fall
gone irrevocably by, *so long*, he'd say
and they knew they could leave.

Family, sometimes a friend from war.
It was always summer. He'd stroll
to the curb and lean heavy
on the car while they started up.
We'd stand with Mom like tulips
against the wooden porch and wave.

Those days my cousins and I talked sex
and God and bragged about our Dads.
We'd hang around, holding up the family name.
Sometimes our folks would all sit down
together over World War II, all eyes
turned inside and far away. *You kids,*
almost without speaking.
We'd all be scared when they'd talk that way.

Tell us, we'd beg, wanting to know
some horrible secret that made them old.

One August we grew tragic, walked
along the beach kicking sand
pretending it was sea. We'd all
fallen for love, got drunk, gone
all the way. We knew
we'd fallen short so long it mattered now.

Uncle Adolph died and the one collecting
junk in Flasher. Mom felt bad
she wouldn't drink his coffee.
Suitcase shabby, Jenny Rose came out
and Uncle Roland lost it again
flying the same plane as '44.
Dave drove down his cycle and weeks
after I wished I was a hood. Dad
looked older, less hair and wouldn't talk
about his brother writing the weird book
to save the world. Mom was appalled
at the relatives and Dad smoked alone,
said goodbye less and less. So long now
it seems all one summer.

## Fishing

The warmest waters beckon
and blind. Once I believed
time could be owned, returned to,
that I could find my childhood
the way I find a grave.

A man fishes all day beneath the sun.
He could be my father leaving
the river, body like a tree,
the root invisible, come to rest
in the sparse farmyard remembered
as it was before the burial.
No name to touch him, his face
becomes a star
and three white horses follow.

I consider the peril of any relation, hooks
caught in the lip of the eyeless
trout, living off its entrails.

In the tea-colored afternoon,
a man walks toward dusk.
He carries a basket, three
silver fish, their open mouths
pools of milk in the dark.
It might be August
or Christmas, the toothed faces
of the aster, blooming,

the tide of the man
flooding an acre of tamarack.
He sees only the light leaving
the valley. In the absence,
his soul like a bell.

Fishing demands belief:
the line cast out
reeled back again.

## The Secret Boats

every daughter hides, every son.
The miles peel back to when
we were all smaller in the time left
on the spreading porch with its black screens
and peonies clumped, bright-faced
beside the steps. Sometimes in the middle
of a womb-like year, a year of rain
and changing light in the afternoon,
I recall my mother's face. How she'd pray

my soul to keep and tell me heaven
was water and angels swam
with wings. I thought I heard them
their smooth stroking
right into my room. Together we'd lie down
on the big bed, a cloud of green
chenille like an ocean under us,
an ocean moving inside,
voices of saints in our ears, caught
on the toothed shore.

Sometimes we'd sleep for hours,
breath floating out, invisible
mermaids in a garden of bees,
mother hanging wash like clippered sails.
Beneath those tents I could be

the Queen of Sheba, land-locked
in waves of snowcapped dandelions.

From the lake of a wooden sandbox
I watch my mother watching clouds.
She is calling me now.
Sometimes I cannot hear
my breath against the truth of her body,
I cannot walk without her
softness in my sleep. Sometimes together
we let them go out of the body.
Like a newborn, one and then another.

(for my mother)

## The Dream Pony

After the moonlight break, after swallowing up
the black and the brown and the white
solid colors of your days,
a dappled one floats down to graze alone
in the northern pasture. She is a mixture
of earth and snow. She is a context
for the twin birds of separation,
a blur, a map of the new world.
As if in answer, she lifts her head
like a silent violin over the ragged weeds
and enters the river
and for a moment the gray air swells
with the fluttering dance of horse.

(for Richard Hugo)

## Far-off Water Movement

This morning, afraid to write,
I come to the smallest room in the house,
closet for belly and toe,
nakedness I never paid much attention
like a waterfall, a cream-colored wall.

With each bath I draw toward healing.
Like the poem rich in clarity,
hint of green poking through snowmelt
collecting what is familiar: dust,
lone words flaking, softening like lumps of soap.

Beyond thin walls,
the faulty hum of neon
continual whoosh and slam of cars
suggest far-off water movement.
I am nowhere near the sea.

Thinking nothing of it,
traffic drowning
inside, I feel the missing breast,
water slowly filling
what is empty.

2

## Breath

The small lake frozen
in its heart of pine
snow flowers.
Bits of fur and ear
embroidered red
in sunlight—
a rabbit's footprint
gouged by a larger
animal.

On the changed lake, we float
like puffs of air
over the stubborn, red weeds of winter.
Something like a fish moves in ice
searching
the way we love what feeds
the owl of our wondering.

(for Lee Bassett)

## Years Later Crows Write Our Letters

Wandering the field, I saw them
carving air into your passionate writing,
worn feathers unraveling
memory of your falling hair
until your crown shone
with the omniscience of fathers.
In the farthest loop, twin beaks
feed black through our names—
uncertain signatures,
the beginning page camouflaged
like reversed weather. Love's closure
clouds the family of letters.

In the same way the family tree
is hidden from the family. It seems the baby
rocks in air, cradled by blackbirds,
shadowed by wings, key
to our troubled syntax.

Death unlocks the letter dreamed.
Count with me the number of steps to the sea.
It is a fierce science—love
drifts out of our eyes.

## Visit

Coming halfway
to your house hidden by trees
I meet the maiden of afternoon
and am deceived:
one of two bold girls embracing
on the lip of summer,
stung in passing.
One eats leftover light,
spitting the pig-eyed jewel.
The other feeds
a cardinal stain.
Which am I?

Tonight, mother answers.
I am as old
as I remember her, uncertain,
hungry for love.
The skinny girl
calls and calls across the plain,
sweet dark melon
lost thirty years ago
unspoiled, covered with willow leaves.

Of two sisters
one is always the watcher,
one is the dancer.
                    —Louise Gluck

## Damages

How often I have watched you dance
whirling tatters of lace
into a rhythm I ache to follow,
slipping like a troubled thought
from my chair in the balcony
as if I'd won a prize
and my name were called
across the velvet dark.

In the first hour
my feet are like stones.
Shadows lock arms,
askew against the blind's
crippled slats.

When we were girls together,
the rose lamps of our breasts
swayed in the night of a tiny room.
Tonight we cannot control the dark
skirt that swirls
around our legs.

## Three Graveyards

### I

The first is close to home
in a small town
filled with bridal wreath
braided by wind.
The stones seem unreal.

### II

This one I have never seen.
It belongs to my husband
who found it one day
in a backward glance.
Overgrown with basswood
it disappears
each June in green.
In rain it glistens
a stone smile,
softly rounded doors
with indecipherable writing.

### III

Wedged against a mountain
two solitary graves,

a vacant house
Someone I love plays there,
a young girl skipping on the marble stones.
She holds a willow branch
green in her palm
and almost catches
my eye.

(for Lois Martin)

# Trying on Hats

Sycamore leaves scrape the sidewalk,
pushed by wind
and I think of tiny, dried amputated hands
and how little I know.
This afternoon in class I spoke of competition.
Now, shy and talkative in your upstairs room
I wallow in a rivalry of hats—

blood velvet shaped like a crown,
a laurel wreath cobwebbed
with tiny plastic lemons netted like flies,
the black plush homburg spouting
a pheasant feather like a striped tongue
circled by rhinestone teeth.

In the mirror I am seduced into changing
as easily as playing cards.
You try too, toying with time
beneath the brim of a mohair creation.
We pretend to move forward and backward in our lives
as though we were machines
and could remember.

That war was before my time.
*Mother never said in which room I was born.*

She adored these hats—look,
twenty-five dollars in 1926 at Steingold Chapman.

At Herbst Department Store, Mother and I
tried on hats, lifting them like brilliant éclairs
from the grey foam stands.
Rainbow was the guiding principle—
mother favoring cornflower blue and white
while I dabbled in peach, chartreuse, purple.

Wordless, we return them to dusty boxes
like fallen planets.
An ostrich feather flutters and curls in tissue,
preserved like a snatch of conversation
meaningless out of context.

In class today a woman said to no one
she was lonely from it
and so were men.
We tried on various ideas, parading,
and suffered through the talk,
the rustle of falling leaves
like seasonal applause.

(for Mary Jenison)

## One Friday Night in Late September

lush with the whir of cicadas,
seductive auto groan,
I hear the sharp duet of leather heels

on concrete. The sound grows near
as if to call me out in lip-soft air
and then retreats in echoing.

I find myself awake and peering
through the black screen.
Framed by the sagging porch

a young couple strolls the naked pavement,
hair powdered with moonlight.
Sensing the invisible muscle,

I watch with longing
as they tenderly carry the thin, brilliant
flags of their jackets.

Frozen in puddled lamplight,
holding hands like children,
already darkening.

(for Dr. George)

## The Empty House on Highway 59

When you came here it was empty
like you
of the hope of children.
Painted pale yellow on the south side
the rest peeling white, grayed with exhaust,
it matched your indecision.
You were free to love

the empty sound wind made
in your head. Time and again
you walked past the house and stared.
It was August and clammy.
The new shirt stuck to your back
and half-moons of sweat
appeared under your arms, rising
when you waved to truckers
barreling through toward Des Moines.

Perhaps you sensed the meager neon
from the one motel
alive in the clouded windows
like flickering tongues in the night,
a mouth
you kissed once.

## Night for Feeding

We walk away like ghosts
in night snow,
the road fallen away, soft sides
tunneling the gorge.
Our feet follow without sound.

My hand floats a small moon
into yours, palm cupped,
blood beating the air between.
The big house sleeps
and we are free to pass through
the gate unseen
having lost all color and age.
Far off, cottonwoods stand guard.

We come for hay,
two horses walking out of night
for feeding, snow
islands on their backs, flying up
from the tangled manes.

(for Art)

## When Paths Cross in a Vacant Lot

If you follow one without logic, seeing
how close you come to losing
your way, and how little it matters
in the journey, the other appears
when you need it least
like a previous life
or a first husband. *Hello*, you say
and try to go on as though
nothing happened. The house of cards,
fragile to begin with, tumbles
from the psychic's hand
into separate days, each a golden ring
along this path. After dark
the problem is imaginary.
But now, in broad daylight
nothing seems casual.
Not the wrinkled grass
nor the stones scuffed with fine summer
dust. Eventually the truth will settle
for staying the same—for better,
for worse, and you will kiss
the precise star
of intersection. Keep moving.
If you stop to rest, your footprints disrobe,
the thread of the moment frays
and breaks, each half another path
knotting all boundaries.

## Autumn Parallax

Leaves drop aimlessly through the month
I was born,
my mother pregnant in autumn,
yellow light going south.

She turns her cheek slightly,
powder drifting into sun.
A whisper of net keeps her face hidden
and from within her dark
pupil opens. Never closer to her heart
I pause with her beside a standing train.

Pieces of sky, blue dust, leave the station
when my father waves. Not farewell
but distance like China
held to the lips of one who had broken
anything or away.
His lover—the space between two wars.
Mine the ties I follow wrong.

A field of snow allows the few
slight weeds of summer, odd
from a window where seasons matter.
*There comes a moment when everything*
*stands still and ripens.*
We are moving and confined
the way leaves dance without leaving
their small circle of air.

3

## Into the Forest, into the Heart

I

I was four when my mother said
I could not touch her breasts, forbidden
as the orchid.
They were soft, like pillows.
My brother and I dreamed
we had some. We drew them
magenta, on paper the color of cream.
We gave breasts to everyone.

That summer we pioneered the neighborhood,
selling visions. Smoke-eaters, we forgave
the meanests kids, believing the inner ear
to be the heart. In the eye of the forest
Baba Yaga's house rose up
on its chicken legs, glutted
with stolen children, their cries
staining the needled floor.
Our words flew up, dark fans

between the shed and garage
where we confessed to each white face:

*She'll come for you sleeping.*
*Her memory is rock. Your mother*
*will remember you dead.*

The pact, then, with blood.

We search now in bodies of our own,
the vein we opened as children healed
to a faint scar.
The blood we share will not suffice.
It cannot feed
the deadly flower. She waits
for each of us to come alone.
Sleep will come when we have cut
and pressed her scent.


II

I meet her bleeding from the heart
in churches or wherever
daughters mourn their mothers. Years
I would not think of her
until she turned in her pillar of salt,
the stems of her arms growing soft.
I feared then, she would overflow
me in a breach of love. What
if I turned her back

[ 38 ]

to the smoking ruins? What
deliverance from men who thought
me sad or mean, who loved
her locked inside, fixed
like that in final passion?
I could be the coldest angel
with breasts of ice
and save them all.
Though hard,
my heart would keep forever.

She sways, lovely, in some valley.
A ghost lifts me, body and all,
in dream and I speak of her
in babble my husband can't understand.
He waits on me like a brother
though his touch admits. Deny her
and she will make an anniversary of her death.
For each imitation, a severed head,
a petal blown in warning
from the bloodless shell. The house
you say is burning is my own.
Better to meet her there,
to know her power,
her softness, as the milk
of disaster,
than meet her when a daughter
or a mother dies, her opened blouse.

## Roses, Lilacs, Poppies

I stole them in broad daylight
to prove I was mean.
Other kids swore truer
when they saw my hands bleed.

My father was quiet and sometimes unhappy.
My mother sulked
and picked raspberries, pulled beets.
Dad mended our back fence
and burned an acre of trash.
Summers at dusk he'd call us home
—*you kids*, and we were his.
Mom he called Josie and loved.
She was pretty then and baked pies,
lemon meringue and homemade apple
that made Dad think he dreamed
them in the war.

My mother grays,
her face changing into her mother's.
The sorrow of farms does not calm.
I refuse my life like cream
and even dead
my father loves me.

I wept when others wept,
buried the dead animals under lilacs

when earwigs curled the leaves.
Mother said it would stink.

Once I lied and Mr. Wilson knew.
I played with his old plow and didn't ask.
Something broke.
*CarolAnn*, he said like my father in my dreams.
I was ashamed and so I hated him
in his snuff-stained shirt.
He never told, though I stole
his flowers and his wife cried.
Behind his back I called him old,
making fun of his suspenders,
the way his shoes flopped open
like slippers in wet grass.
He still jawed with Dad
and tipped a white hat to Mom Saturdays.
Just a farmer from Missouri, come west.
I couldn't know he came to die,
his poppies bursting orange every spring.

I lied and lied.
The *Rialto*, black and white movie,
a blond woman in her slip screaming
*you bastard*, slapping the man dead.
Stealing money and telling my friends
I prayed. If being beautiful was love
I wanted to be mugged. *No*,
I said until they let me be.

## The Talking Doll

A thousand stitchings
ricochet in your dream of her
gypsy hair. She hungers
for the purple berry tangled in leaves,
crawling though a wall of teeth.
She is the seed lost
one afternoon the forest moved inside
and you never went home.
So lost you forgot who you were,
turning blonder and blonder.
Little kick-in-the-stomach, she cuts
like mirrors, arcs
deep in blue forbidden dream.

Ask her, why
the rose in the spider's eye
and why women smother
their flowering bodies
in star quilts smelling of attics
in North Dakota and Iowa,
breathing through the needle's bright eye.

In the cauldron, the gaping buggy,
you are kissing yourself awake,
the dangerous doll

telling the random story from childhood
in the ancient courtroom of toys:

the blond doll slicing her curls
the bald doll dancing on bloody toes
the dead doll clogged with tears.

So long you have been whispering your name
there are times when you are all there is.

## What I Said

I could say I have come to visit, knowing
the preserves must be opened
and the sweet jam taken in
with the dark tea. You open
the frail door
and take me to sit beside you. I lean
into the grain of your table, leaving
no mark you would ever remember
into a future that could be
only yours. No wife,
no mother can see you so clearly,
butter sun spilling from your palm,
knotting its secret heart
into the wood's calm face. *Familiar*

was what I said instead of *love*, wanting
the sad truth of family
to descend through my slightly open mouth
like a portion of bread taken
with honey tea. However early, the sun
is falling. I know this.
What loveliness holds me now in firm arms
will remain until night sends me away.
On the table before us
a feathered ear of wheat bends
in glass against
the grain of our meeting.

## Into Our Hands

After the beating of walls
and the stuttering flowers of anger
I am hiding, plasmic
in the orchard, wearing only
my white nightgown.
Tonight is impossible to save.
Take my hand,
plum leaf in shadow,
knotted bird
on whose back I fly
between lines of porch light.
In this valley I can teach you anything—
star bath of cruelty,
blue ice in the bowl.
Lie down with me.
White breath of cottonwood showers us
with tiny clouds of seed,
bright cricket
and spirit slipping
into our hands.

## Outcast

I found your face in mine. Once
you kissed me in public (or did not)
dreamed me (or did not)
and I was. In your one slipping of love
the day, the night you wanted me
I scarcely saw.

So much is needed: that lie
masquerades as dire principle. Lonely,
all are afraid. Home
crouches before them, lion or dog
and yet they climb.

You do not willingly go, and I
am shamed. In some other life, some country
where scars are beautiful, we
save ourselves for graves, withholding

love. The day that word was wrong
my mouth went blue. I turn back
the mountain. None gives truly to another:
hill, skull and rose.

## The Double Axe

Proof how the ritual kiss
glides deep
like a ring slipped on a finger
or an unborn child
in the blood-warm water.

## Storm

Perhaps the lover in sleep
who speaks for us
the glossolalia of rage and desire
fades when scrutinized
like the breath of violence
in civil conversation.
Returned to talking to ourselves
aloud in rooms
we double back, dreaming
the blood sound.
If we are naked and willing,
arm in arm we enter
the inarticulate circus
with its guttural menagerie
and sequined women shattering air.

## Ibeji

Before I carve him from wood
he is a man
who loves me, who knows
my secret name.
I am looking into the round mirror
in my parent's room.
I do not yet bleed.
My hair drips from the bath
and with shaking fingers
I part it on one side—it is short
and my mother's yellow comb
creates waves in the blackness
until all I can make out
is his face. Slowly I lean
toward the heat,
his breath clouding
my reflection.
I am afraid someone will come in
and notice him there
in my body, insisting
that I speak.

I carve him from wood.
When men kiss my breasts
pain loosens,
crumbling like an aged photograph.
I say the name aloud.
In the mirror all is as before:
root, artery, bone.

(for Robert Johnson)

# The Red Envelope

comes to us empty,
unexpected as pain in the left arm
driving to work and the light
bird in the chest wakens
from its rhythmic rocking
to flutter toward the throat,
or the child we believed in
turns for the first time.
As an old friend
dead or forgotten
it arrives, following lines
on our faces, singing
its wolf-song.

In Minnesota wolves are silver.
A moon sound comes out of them,
feathering snow endlessly down
into the red mouth
hiding its true color
as though it were a life
we are trying to forget.
Always with a promise
a neatly squared opening,
a sound to hide or reveal
what we barely remember
the moment it is wrenched from the body.

4

## Sophia Apollonia

In any door
I stand and wave goodbye
to an unknown figure leaving my house.
Embarrassed claim on the stranger
shouts back a poverty that binds.
The record shows eight sons,
the last born perfectly still
the moment of your death.
You left them all children.
Even the house slept in monotonous purity,
a grieving that could not last.

When we return, grass ruts the foundation.
We bring no seed
but a red wind to track
the invisible frame.
Pops is dead and one son gone crazy
flying his bomber every dream
since the war. I am ten
and scared of falling.
But Dad and I know it matters
to look into the grave.
We track each slender sign into the night.

In the naked flesh-mass exists a real man
of no titles. He is always coming in
and out through your sense organs. If
you don't know him yet, look!

—Rinzai


## A Real Man of No Titles


He comes out when the last great aunt
has gone to sleep on the farm
no one in the family will admit
is ours, barn broken down
garden gone to weed where we stood
twenty years ago for pictures.

I know he reads Grandpa's dirty books.
I know he is knitting
the family history as afghan,
alcoholic uncles and all. He
hounds the chicken coop where I played dolls
and pioneers, the nutmeg wild
in his hair. Where my brother, John
drove the jeep into the ground
he pauses, remembering how guilt
is born. I follow him

far. Over one and one-half miles to the next farm
another brother's land goes brown.
I played there too, undressing the china doll,
her sawdust legs naked

in clover. The velvet bonnet is still
lost. So many dog-days I carried
lunch to imaginary men working
that sad field.

He comes for my sister
shunned by Grandma one whole summer
she had no friends. No boys believed
in that hick town. I hope they skate
on wooden wheels to hell. She walked
me out nights to pee,
our long gowns shimmering
past the windbreak.

He is the bogey man
who gave bride books and hearts
to little girls, the one I watched for
all the years I ran home from school.
He is the bum that Mom fed
and regretted for twenty years. The one
that made Dad love her long
after she'd forgotten and the trains
quit and we moved to the right side.

He went to war. Sad man
came home and we were born.
Old Joe was black and dying long before
and Red Wing still waits on my wall.
That man of no titles is real
like chickens were
and the big board fence is not.

## For All You Know

You choose a day
and ride it close as a daughter,
loyal to invisible
hairs on the arm of a small-boned girl.
At home in the glitter of a five-and-dime
you are worth it,
young again and freely stupid,
wearing white on a dark day
like a flag. To go from here

means pain, your guard let down,
the childhood farm
where all the animals have been eaten
or sold. Grandpa never loved the barn
and Grandma gives her past away
like someone else's china.
Where you played house in the machine shed
it was oil you smelled, not grain.
You knew the truth about the humpbacked chicken
    coop.
From the doorway
far stairs rippled in grass.

It seemed yellow horses galloped
the twister down Johnny's field,
leaving everything unchanged.
Ten years your uncle
stalks that gray mouth in every bottle,

rising and falling with the backbone of his life.
The perfectly ugly August
his dream touched down
high winds buckled the tracks, drove
straw through fence poles.
You might have surrendered to learn
it never leaves, the calm
riding the same twisted rail.

## Abandoned Farm

Nothing kisses wind in empty rooms.
I hear a river,
snow water and cistern,
gentle piss of girls squatting in grass.
In the mouths of cows
cud becomes a blue thread of milk
unwinding, crows
turning air around the barn.

We roll over and over in the hay,
swinging on the knotted rope
out the window.
Whatever we want, we dream—
horses, boys, red velvet dresses.

The white farmhouse is far from town.
At the skating rink we get inside the music
racing what we know
around the concrete, fenced-in field
we think is heaven
but is an emptiness we fill
like our mothers and grandmothers
for awhile, in a small town.

(for Renee Peterson)

## Understanding Tornadoes

In time, I will climb the stairs
easily, believing geometry—
old lovers joined
on truth's blackboard
in a room filled with chalk-dust.
Each step begets a theorem
from the past. I think
and circle back, touching the puzzle.
Bald Mr. Downs has taken off his coat.
We are about to learn something.
We gaze out windows in the airless classroom
blowing a kiss beyond the green
square of schoolyard, its pretense
of field, to the far farms
of Dakota and Montana.
I make a field. Grandfather is there
in his pin-striped overalls
and death is out of the question.
A bright shape on the horizon
waves something like arms.
Black clouds lumber our way.
Though a child
I, too, am in the field
and open to rain. Mr. Downs
says the circle is a field.

He cuts it in two
and two again. The center

holds like a tiny eye
swimming in bits of chalk,
trying to blink them away.
Once Dad got metal slivers
in his eye. Is this what I am
learning? I shut my eyes
tight like a fist, and the green
and red circles burst
in the velvet nothing where
heartbeat rules. I am air
and this is high school.
Figures appear and are erased
hour after hour on the slate board,
each line, prescience of rain.
In this room of dust and light
each step proved withstands
the test. What's left
but a wish for another way
to center that staring eye
conjured by numbers
the teacher says we dream?

## Photo of Women Plowing

(circa 1899)

The driver's face has no features,
a dark day–moon
above eight women harnessed to the plow.
They do not look up or talk
of beauty wrapped in cotton.
They hide their eyes
in bonnets, nothing certain
but the driver, slow
and heavy-booted.
They know they are better than horses.
They have eaten silence
with chapped lips at table,
more bitter before son
or husband than this boss man.
His face blackens from too few words.

Under billowed skirts, soft
forms blur the ugliest field. Wind
melds with grain dust, and moths
fly up suddenly at night
when the women wash their legs
lifting them softly in the half
light behind the shed.

## Plain in Level Grass

The clocks have gathered in my face,
planted long sounds in my head.
I hear women walk in low fields,
break their hands, spread
them dark and plain in level grass.
They speak softly of their men
who ride out summer on cold plows,
open the ground, mount the sky,
thick arms reaping the sun.

I hear their breasts calling
in dull cotton dresses, low tones
sowing rain, discontent, an early dusk
to bring the men striding to the porch
and finally to bed. Their solid bodies
roll in the low fields, heavy
with the smell of horses, new-mown hay
marking time, marking time
between the long legs of their wives.

## The Train Always Goes Home

I have taken the train that always goes home:
we are one in the humming steel.
Desire and dust marry the farm.

Come as a child, a kiss to that farm,
pretend to know what is real.
I have taken the train that always goes home.

A ghost waits in wind, ground home
by a sky whose blue won't heal
desire and dust. Marry the farm

where rain-filled cattle protect from harm
the child who, circling, encounters the real.
I have taken the train that always goes home.

Plow scars and alfalfa, anchor that home
in an ocean of quivering steel.
Desire and dust marry the farm,

let the earth go by. Quack-grass or home
let it happen, let it wound and heal.
I have taken the train that always goes home.
Desire and dust marry the farm.

## Locksmith

Now the door has swung
inward to exclude even old friends.
You feel your way with your fingertips,
something slipping into place
like a fertilized egg
making its single, blind pilgrimage
to the womb.
                    In its cave
even love freezes
unresponsive. Entering,
you crave all exits like a priest,
the circles of ritual
and possession. Metal teeth unclench
for the same skeleton—
the shape of your own
catching at last.

5

I wanted to write about coming west, falling
from grace, good neighborhoods
to bad, divorce and poetry. But none
of this is news. Death
does not come from east to west
or always in the afternoon. It can happen
best in cars, the people fancy
and holding hands. It happened
to da Vinci's "Last Supper"
molding in Milan, the resin giving in
to smog on the wall of the Santa Maria
alle Grazie Church. It can be written,
as weather here is too often scattered, sunsets
turning thunder in the contiguous states.
No season is right for dying
or fishing. For truth I look in the papers:
the famous fresco now a supper
for mold. It all begins peacably enough.

(for Jon Eastman)

## The Brown-Headed Cowbird
## Has a Blue, Blue Tongue

A brief invasion—storm, remembered love
when bridges were there to wave from
and winding paths ended nowhere sad.
We were smiling then and growing blind
the way we do when life runs good
for years, when everyone's alive.

Blue sky seldom rains. Somewhere lovers
are leaving only to return, come spring.
Come fall, they promenade through cloud.
Where the Blackfoot flows along a dusty road
dogs are glad to leave the town behind.
Arm in arm we walk the razor streets
to all we must become. Come clean

and turn to stone. The brown-headed cowbird
has a blue, blue tongue. A muddy river runs
for years through plain and empty field.
Happy people know they want it all,

learn to trust their own deaf ear.
A girl, ignorant of farms, her words blond,
her hair true, leaves you as you were—
a crow's-wing pretty with her man. Call in
your life, the smallest tip of finger left

behind, the rusted blade a dying threat.
When you decide you've had enough, slam
the rotten door hard for every lonely year.
No one dies of thirst who watches
cities burn but they die just the same.

(for Richard Hugo)

## The Beauty of Animals

In the feedlot modern farmers talk.
No matter how lonely

they fatten pigs and cows
for eventual disassembly.

They perform logical operations.
I am dreaming of starvation,

of animals coming into our world.
There is so little of us left

in their eyes, pools of rain.
We are one heaving body, breath

rising in the open pasture.
Silent in the barn,

we sink heavy as stone
stunned by the blow.

## Independence Day on the
## Flathead Reservation

Today, outside the Arlee Post Office I was cold.
I saw an Indian veteran, naked—
no medals and without a gun. Something
like a knife, his face

an invisible burn.
His lips faltered with words
that mumbled past, broken feathers
entreating wind, crumbling into ashes

smearing their bitter ink.
My face burned white in the heat. Watching
the forgotten language
drift and curl between us like the

fine ceremonial dust between our toes
I drew closer to him.

## La Chingada

is a girl I know
who drinks the eyes of men
like gray water.
When flesh burns,
men trade their tongues
for a single night.
Ash-skinned babies
fall from her body, cold
like the pale river
men seek at death.
In the dawn of Cihuacoátl,
she leaves them
blind, dumb
praying to virgin saints.

# Memory of Trees

Leaves are letting go,
a cloud of maples burning.
Some may never turn
this way again. Some
are naked already.

The falling is everywhere, so gradual
even the trees have forgotten
the pewter gaze of sky, unflinching
through miles of snow.

Once you left me
at the foot of a mountain
to bring up a day's water.
Your gesture is all I have,
straws of your being.
Do the eyes dream? Through the haze,
brilliant skin of the birches.

## A Vase of Flowers

(after a painting by Melanie de Comoléra)

Victorian, they dissemble at first—
the poppies ruddy with health
and the pansies, insipid but virtuous.
What permits a closer look
are the pinched lips of the roses, sallow
like mouths of young whores
after shooting up on their nights off.
In its own way, each breathes
beyond the tangle of arrangement.
We could be driving down sharp streets
in Minneapolis or Akron
when it happens,
the offer of an hour's trick
or the painter's life, too accurate
to hold us through this sad century.

## Hearing the Retarded Sing

It was because you heard them sing
that you wrote on Jimmy's bare chest

with the magic marker: Jimmy can dress himself,
Jimmy can feed himself, Jimmy can

go to the toilet by himself. One
night when dark covered your mouth

like a gigantic hand you listened
to what was out there, a sound

coming toward you dressed like Halloween
in a retarded man's body: *You are*

*my sunshine, my only sunshine*

a split second when silence
coils still and cool as a cobra

in the heart, rising
until your throat aches.

(for Tom Blow)

## Solitary Song for Black Brother Gone Home

Think of me, big brother, when you slide on down
to the Sunset Lounge for conversation
and some smoke, when you're broke
and ready for the road—Chicago
or New York, think of me
the way I think of you on the avenue
alone and no woman
to call you home

so when you sleep your thankful hour
shooting through air
or keep vigil on the floor
of a sad waiting room
treading dust in the generous cosmos
we call home in spite
of state lines and liner lies
think of me

think again of the moon in Omaha
the zero of laughter in Omaha
all rising, all ashes
between black borders and breakfast
at The Fair Deal (where it is)
where Saturday mornings jig

to the tune of two weird calendars
calling us home

big brother, when you slip off
those traveling shoes and stretch
your old black toes
and the years line up like face cards
think of me undertaking the worn edges
putting them softly to rest.

(for Etheridge Knight)

## Burning the Sweatlodge

You talk of time,
the fifteen uncreative guys
still in your hometown
waiting for you to never leave,
the sad father
who loves you for your fear,
the mother gone softly incognito with grief,
distant as rain
in bourbon-colored elms.
Each leaf turns, then falls

like an adopted child
when it is time.
Tonight you are lost in my living room.
I give you my guitar to play

against that abstract enemy.
We sing.
The sweatlodge burns,
filling our eyes with smoke
the shape of funerals,
wedding
our emptiness
with what is imagined.

(for Jeremiah McSparron)

[ 78 ]

## Notes

"La Chingada": Cihuacoátl is an ancient Aztec earth-goddess who, today, in rural Mexico is associated with the legend of *la llorona*, a weeping woman who cries out in the night.

"Photo of Women Plowing": The original photo is contained in the Saskatchewan Archives, University of Regina.

"Autumn Parallax": "There comes a time when everything stands still and ripens." From "Grappa in September," *Hard Labor* by Cesare Pavese.

CarolAnn Russell was born in North Dakota and grew up in Bozeman, Montana and Detroit Lakes, Minnesota. She graduated from St. Cloud State University and received her M.A. and M.F.A. degrees from the University of Montana, where she studied in the Montana Writers Workshop with Madeline DeFrees and Richard Hugo.

In addition to serving as poetry editor of *Cutbank* and coeditor of *GiltEdge, New Series*, she has been an NEA author-in-residence and a Fulbright finalist. From 1981 to 1985, she was assistant professor and writer-in-residence at Tarkio College in Missouri. In 1985 she moved to the University of Nebraska–Lincoln, where she is a Ph.D. candidate. Her work has appeared in many journals and anthologies over the past ten years.

*Photo by Michael Featherston*

[ 81 ]

University Presses of Florida, the agency
of the State of Florida's university system
for publication of scholarly and creative
works, operates under policies adopted by
the Board of Regents. Its offices are located
at 15 Northwest 15th Street, Gainesville,
Florida 32603.


Library of Congress Cataloging-in-Publication Data

Russell, CarolAnn.
    The red envelope.

    (University of Central Florida
contemporary poetry series)
    I. Title.   II. Series.
PS3568.U7656R4   1985   811'.54     85–9163
ISBN 0–8130–0828–X (alk. paper)

[ 83 ]